MW00715422

To,

Aliza

Love.

Pearl Hong

8/18/23

To order additional copies of this book, contact
Toll Free +65 3165 7531 (Singapore)
Toll Free +60 3 3099 4412 (Malaysia)
www.partridgepublishing.com/singapore
orders.singapore@partridgepublishing.com

Because of the dynamic nature of the Internet, any web addresses or links contained in this book may have changed since publication and may no longer be valid. The views expressed in this work are solely those of the author and do not necessarily reflect the views of the publisher, and the publisher hereby disclaims any responsibility for them.

ISBN
ISBN: 978-1-5437-7487-0 (sc)
ISBN: 978-1-5437-7485-6 (e)

Library of Congress Control Number: 2023912680

Printed in Singapore

07/11/2023

PARTRIDGE

AS THERE IS **LOVE**
THERE IS
<u>ABUNDANCE</u>.

AS THERE IS
ABUNDANCE,
THERE IS
<u>ENERGY</u>
AND
<u>CREATIVITY</u>.

LOVE IS NOT
SOMETHING
YOU FIND.
LOVE IS YOUR
NATURAL STATE.

<u>IT IS</u>
<u>WITHIN YOU</u>.

IF YOU WANT THE
BEST LIFE,
DO YOUR BEST
EVERYDAY.
WE ARE JUST
GIVEN WHAT WE
GIVE.

*Always choose
to win in life*

*It is your **responsibility**
to raise your **energy**.*

*Once you have the
insights to dream,
it is a blessing.
It is your inner
voice speaking.*

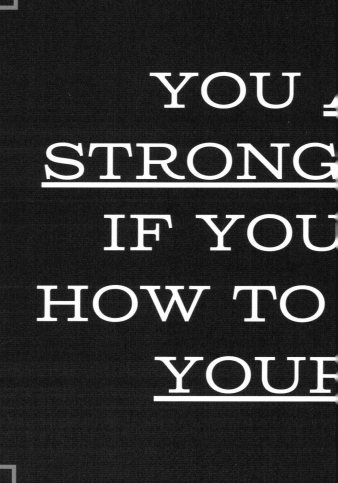

RE A
PERSON
KNOW
CORRECT
SELF.

Maximize the gift of life.

YOU ARE
BLESSED WITH
CREATIVE
THINKING &
INFINITE ENERGY
AS YOU HAVE
YOUR HEART TO
OTHER PEOPLE
GET THEIR
ULTIMATE
LIVES TOO.

WHEN YOUR RELATIONSHIP WITH YOURSELF IS BASED ON LOVE AND RESPECT, YOUR RELATIONSHIP TO EVERYTHING IN YOUR LIFE WILL CHANGE.

LOVE BEGINS WITH YOU.

Your happiness is contagious.

Spread more.

IN EVERY
BREAKTHROUGH
IN YOUR LIFE,
EITHER YOU GET
ONE WISDOM
OR A HUNDRED
OF IT.

IN MANIFESTING,
IT IS HOW YOU
FEEL ABOUT THE
RESULT THAT
YOU DESIRE.

*Your dreams will chase
you by the frequency
and the person you are.*

*Thoughts plus strong
emotion towards your goal
equals **MANIFESTATION**.*

As you aim for progress everyday, it strengthens your discipline.

WHATEVER
YOU WANT,
YOU MUST GIVE;
LIKE JOY, WISDOM,
APPRECIATION,
ENCOURAGEMENT
AND
CONTRIBUTION.

AS YOU TRY
NEW THINGS,
IT IS EITHER
YOU WIN
OR
YOU LEARN.

You have **passion and purpose** in your life, that's why you are unstoppable.

What matters is what you do **TODAY**.

*The secret to real happiness
is progress. Make progress.
That is where we feel alive!*

Your **RESULTS** *may be
CLOSER than you THINK.*

YOUR SOUL ALWAYS SPEAKS ABOUT GREAT AND LIMITLESS POSSIBILITIES.

YOUR DREAMS ARE **POSSIBLE!**

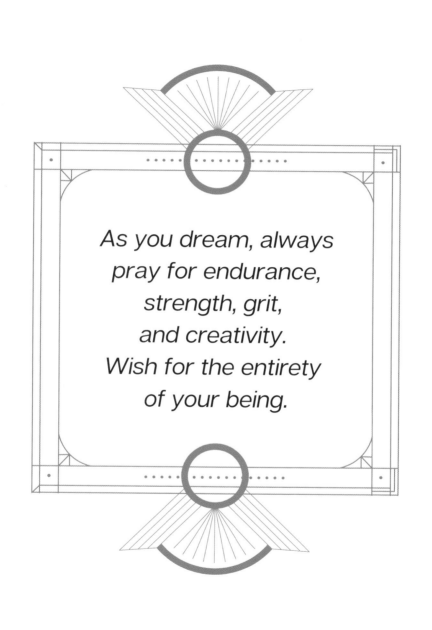

*As you dream, always
pray for endurance,
strength, grit,
and creativity.
Wish for the entirety
of your being.*

KNOW THAT THE WORLD IS **ABUNDANT.**

Your greatest contribution to humanity is your own realization.

As you uplift yourself, you uplift everyone else around you.

LOVE IS NOT
SOMETHING YOU
FIND BECAUSE
IT IS YOUR
NATURAL STATE.

LOVE IS WITHIN YOU.
TALK TO IT, FEEL IT.

YOUR BRAIN IS YOUR POWERHOUSE. FILL IT IN MINDFULLY.

Only say what you want to experience.
*Use **positive words** to reshape your life.*

I direct myself to notice the beautiful things that are happening. That is why my life becomes more beautiful.

The real secret to happiness is **PROGRESS**.

Make the most of your life in a creative and abundant way.

YOU ARE A STRONG PERSON AS YOU KNOW HOW TO <u>CORRECT YOURSELF.</u>

EVERY BREAKDOWN IS A BREAKTHROUGH

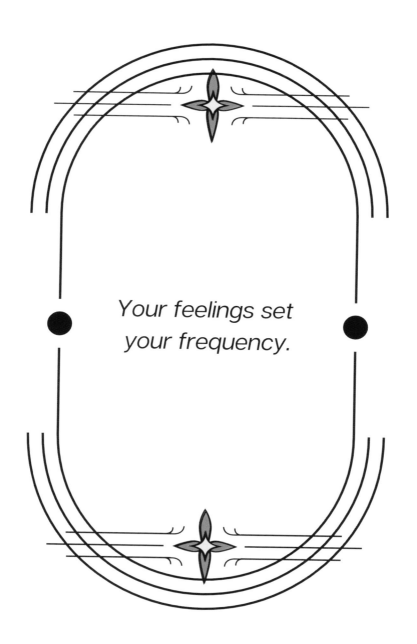

Your feelings set your frequency.

Only say what you
want to experience.
Use positive words to
shape your life.

**As you think happiness
to others, indeed, you are
truly happy yourself.**

DON'T PLEASE HARDER, COMMUNICATE BETTER.

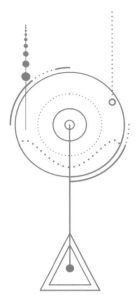

If you want
exceptional results,
act like one.

Always compare yourself with the most **beautiful possibilities.**

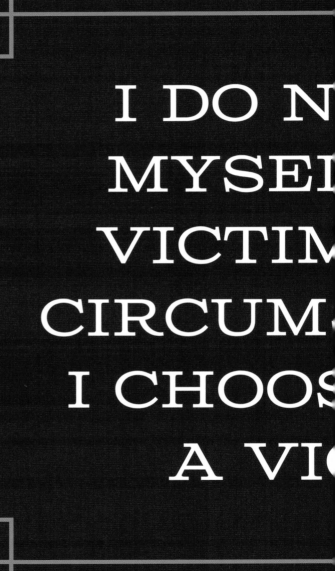

I DO N
MYSEL
VICTIM
CIRCUM
I CHOOS
A VIC

OT SEE

F AS A

OF MY

TANCE,

E TO BE

TOR.

REAL RELATIONSHIP WITH YOURSELF IS THE MOMENT YOU BECOME **REAL** TO YOURSELF.

You need to become what you want to attract.

It starts inside, from your mind, heart and soul. With these, your body will respond to what will be manifested.

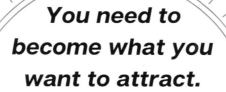

Asking the right questions will give you the right answers.

Happiness is a state of being. Happy people want to bring happiness to other people.

Life
is one big continuous
circle of giving and
receiving energy.

If you believe that you can, the idea of execution will flow into your life.

YOUR MIND
CREATES
YOUR WORLD.

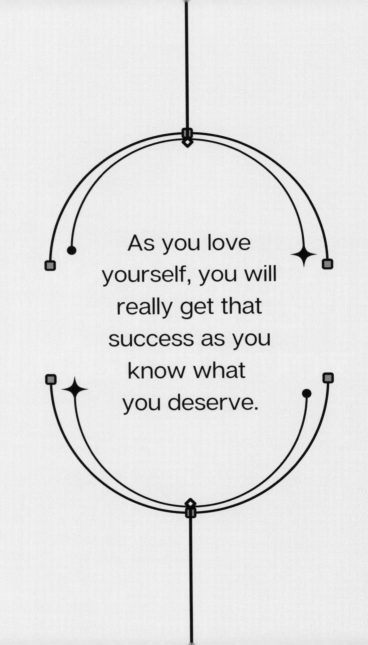

As you love
yourself, you will
really get that
success as you
know what
you deserve.

KNOWLEDGE IS POWER. WISDOM IS KNOWLEDGE APPLIED.

YOU ATTRACT
THOSE PEOPLE
WHO HAVE THE
SAME <u>MINDSET</u>,
SAME <u>PRACTICES</u>,
SAME <u>VALUES</u>
AND SAME
<u>VISION</u>
AS YOURS.

Today's mantra:
I feel so happy
and
I feel so fulfilled!

Transform your life by
changing the way
you see things.

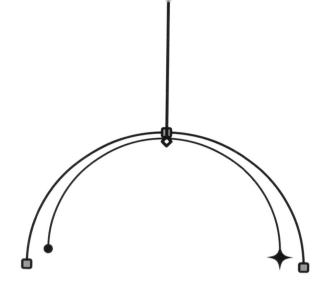

Fulfillment

is the ultimate.

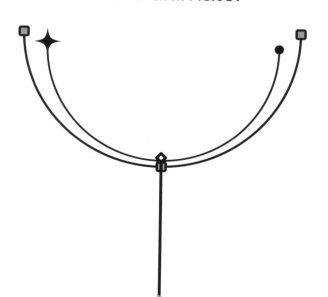

YOUR SELF-TALK IS VERY IMPORTANT.

CONSCIOUSLY SELECT AND CONSUME WHAT YOU NEED AND WHAT YOU THINK IS RIGHT FOR YOUR SOUL. YOU ARE NOT WHAT YOU THINK, YOU ARE THE THINKER.

VIBRATE
LOVE

*If you want to be successful,
you have to love success.
You have to celebrate success.*

*If you are not there yet in success,
celebrate someone who has it. Love
the feeling of someone who has it
and you will attract success.*
Success will love you!

IT TAKES A CERTAIN LEVEL OF **PERSONALITY** AND **MATURITY** FOR YOU TO BE ABLE TO GET THE RESULT THAT YOU WANT.

*People with **great personalities** won many battles.*

Always defend your dreams.

Your thoughts are the determiner of your energy.

Protect your feelings because your feelings will determine what you will magnetize.

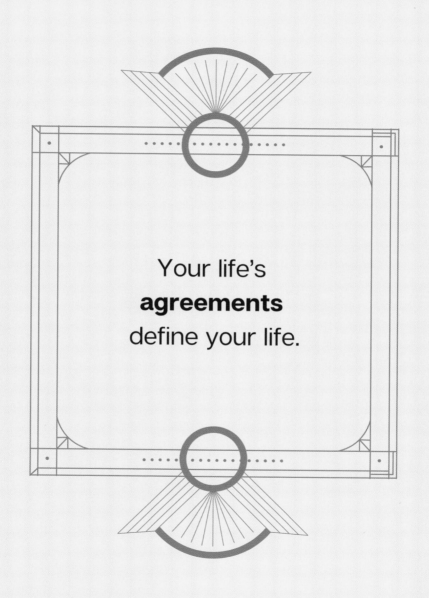

Your life's
agreements
define your life.

LET LIFE
BE YOUR
TEACHER.

EVERYTHING
WE NEED
TO LEARN
EXISTS.
YOU JUST NEED
TO SEE IT.

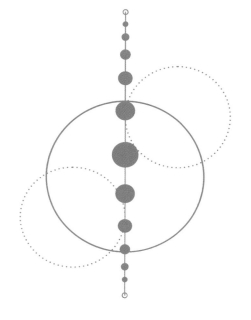

Continue adding value
*to people's lives and
notice how big of a*
positive impact
it will bring.

Humility
+
Awareness
=
SUCCESS

WHEN YOU
COMBINE THE
ABILITY TO
EXPRESS YOUR
UNIQUE TALENT
WITH SERVICE
TO HUMANITY,
YOU WILL MAKE
USE OF YOUR
PURPOSE.

CELEBRATE LIFE BY LIVING IT!

*Do not only do what you love, but also **LOVE** what you do."*

*The finish line is not the title, not the profession.
The finish line is full of intangible things.*
You cannot buy it, but you can gain it.

*What you believe will become **YOU**.*

Gratitude emits feelings of success.

TAKE A JOYFUL
BLAME TO
ASCEND IN LIFE.

SEEK TO BECOME
BETTER AND
YOU WILL BE
SHOWERED WITH
OVERFLOWING
IDEAS,
CREATIVITY
AND ENERGY.

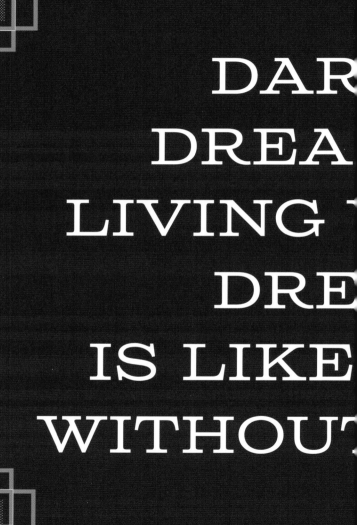

E TO

M BIG!

ITHOUT

AMS

A BODY

A SOUL.

You are what you consume.
Choose where you will
put your energy.
*Be aware of what **content**, **energy**,*
***thoughts** and **words** you consume.*

RADIATE LIGHT

*Seek to become
better and you
will be showered
with overflowing ideas,
creativity and energy.*

*Have the **humility**
to assess yourself.*

INITIATE
GROWTH.

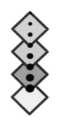

*See everything
wonderfully.*

*The more you
are **mindful**,
the more **wisdom**
you will get in life.*

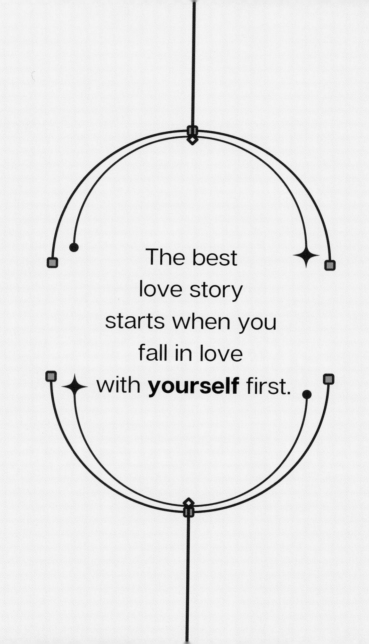

The best
love story
starts when you
fall in love
with **yourself** first.

SMALL GOALS
=
SMALL ACTIONS

BIG GOALS
=
BIG ACTIONS

THE MORE YOU
ARE MINDFUL,
THE MORE
WISDOM YOU
WILL GET IN LIFE.

We are here in this world to
LOVE and to **GROW**.

Your greatest contribution to
humanity is your <u>self-realization.</u>

*Be open to receive
the abundance of life.*

*Your existence is a blessing
as you bless their existence.*

SPEAK
ENCOURAGEMENT

YOUR
WORDS
SHAPE
YOUR
LIFE

GIVING WHAT
YOU HAVE
RECEIVED
MAKES YOUR
SOUL IN **BLISS.**

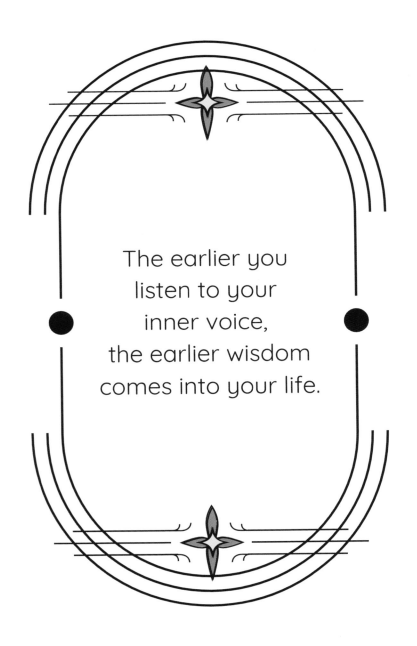

The earlier you
listen to your
inner voice,
the earlier wisdom
comes into your life.

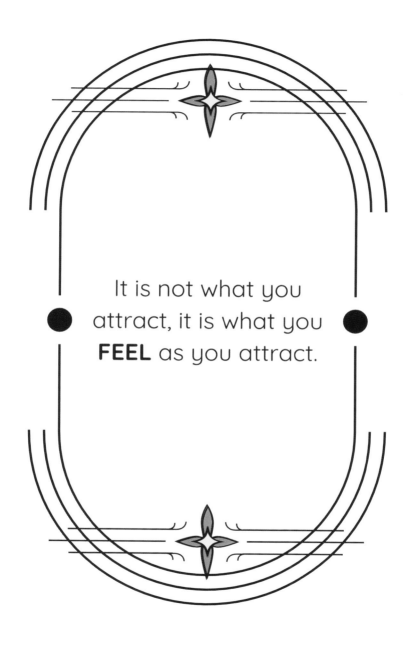

It is not what you attract, it is what you **FEEL** as you attract.

*Have that breakthrough today
as you lift your vibes.*

*When you feel good,
you are aligned with*
ABUNDANCE.

THE UNIVERSE
IS SERVING THE
DESERVING.

IF YOU STRONGLY
BELIEVE THAT
YOU CAN HAVE A
BRIGHT FUTURE,
YOU DIRECT
YOURSELF TO BE
IN THE STATE
OF BEAUTIFUL
POSSIBILITY.

Every idea is a **blessing**.
Execute things
immediately.
Once you get an idea,
execute and
do it right away.

Doing your best everyday makes you fulfilled.

Your consciousness creates your life. Everything you have is what you choose to believe.

EVERY TIME
THERE ARE
CHALLENGES
YOU HAVE THE
CHOICE TO EITHER
RUN FROM IT
OR FACE THEM.
**ALWAYS CHOOSE
TO FACE IT** AND
**BECOME
STRONGER.**

When comparing stops,
your rhythm starts.

Mean no judgment,
only understanding.

THE HIGHEST FREQUENCY IS **LOVE!**

THE EARLIER YOU
LISTEN TO YOUR
INNER VOICE,
THE EARLIER
WISDOM COMES
INTO YOUR LIFE.

Our earth allow us to experience life and discover our fullest potentials.

If the thought or the idea is given to you, it is a blessing, so act on it fast as a respect and gratitude to the blessing.

When you pray, do not just ask for more blessings but ask for more strength and wisdom.

THERE'S REALLY A MATCH OF FREQUENCY. THE REASON WHY YOU HAVE THE LIFE THAT YOU HAVE NOW IS BECAUSE THAT IS WHAT MATCHES YOUR FREQUENCY.

THAT'S THE REASON WHY YOU NEED TO FIX YOUR FREQUENCY SO IT MATCHES WITH YOUR GOALS.

IF YOU
TO BE
SUCCE
CH
IMPROV

WANT
COME
SSFUL,
ASE
EMENT.

HAVE FAITH THAT IT WILL BE GIVEN TO YOU.

You need a dream
to be happy in
your life.

FAILURE AND **REJECTIONS** ARE YOUR ALLY. THEY MAKE YOU **WISER, BRAVER,** AND A **BETTER PERSON** THAN YOU WERE YESTERDAY.

CELEBRATE YOUR LIMITLESS POSSIBILITIES.

WE ARE ALL
CREATED EQUAL.
IT IS UP TO US
HOW WE MAKE
OURSELVES
EXTRAORDINARY.

SPEED AND
ENDURANCE
ARE THE
FOUNDATION
OF ACHIEVING
BIG RESULTS.

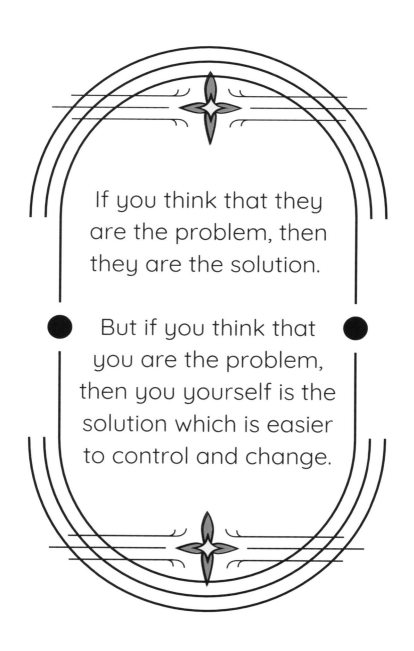

If you think that they are the problem, then they are the solution.

But if you think that you are the problem, then you yourself is the solution which is easier to control and change.

*Exposure to abundance
gives you another mindset and it
makes you dream even more.*

---

*Speak from the heart
because it is your heart that speaks.*

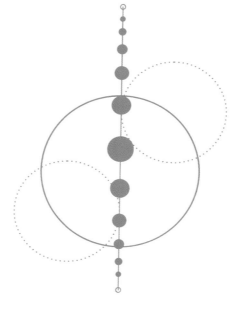

Daily assessment leads to **daily improvements**.

Monthly assessment leads to **monthly improvements**.

Yearly assessment leads to **yearly improvements**.

I WANT YOU
TO LIVE,
NOT JUST
TO EXIST.

Our wishes are always being granted, but not always in a way we expect them to be.

*Have a strong and
a deep purpose*

**Crack yourself,
let the light in,
and expand from within.**

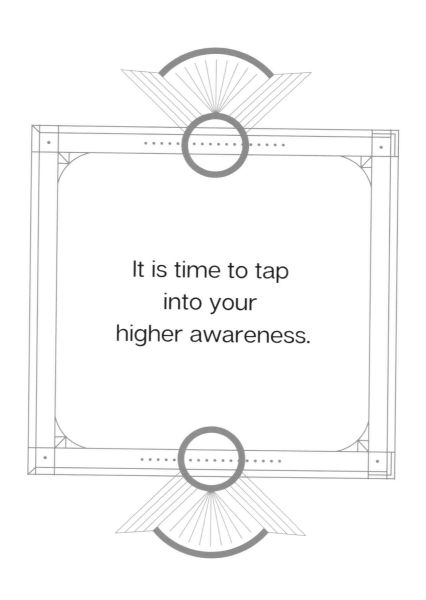

It is time to tap
into your
higher awareness.

YOU ARE A FREE SOUL WITH A FREE WILL.

THAT IS YOUR POWER.

*The problem is not the
problem but it
is the way you see it.*

The good life is the life you create with the choices you make.

Always remember each day presents a new opportunity for you to pursue dreams, conquer goals, and walk on purpose.

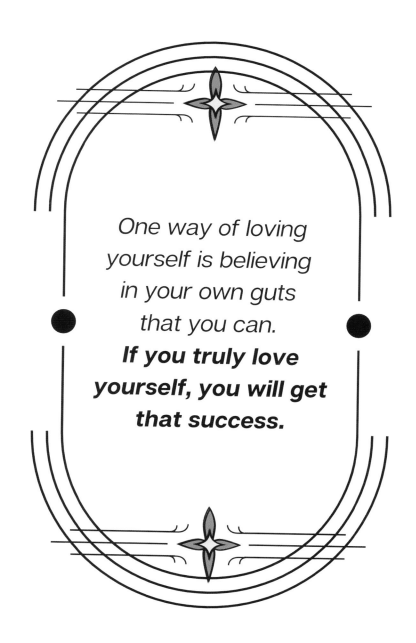

One way of loving
yourself is believing
in your own guts
that you can.
**If you truly love
yourself, you will get
that success.**

YOUR LIFE IS THE SWEETEST IF YOU ARE ALWAYS IN THE STATE OF LOVE, GRATITUDE AND APPRECIATION.

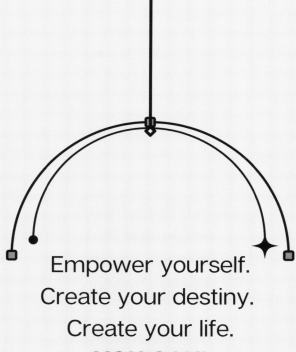

Empower yourself.
Create your destiny.
Create your life.
<u>YOU CAN!</u>

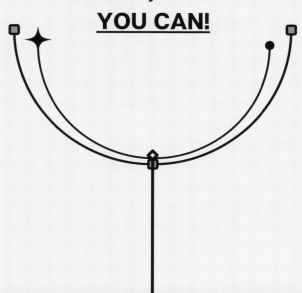

You have a higher self-image and likeness to our Higher Creator.

———✕———

We are equally gifted and powerful. Exercise the power of creation because you are the builder of your own life.

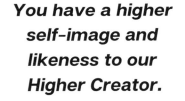

THE PATH IS ALL
YOURS AS LONG
AS YOU ARE
WILLING TO
COMMIT AND ARE
WILLING TO
EXECUTE.

DO YOUR BEST WHILE BEING **PATIENT** ON WHATEVER JOURNEY YOU ARE TAKING.

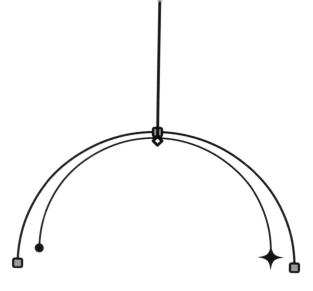

Your <u>ENERGY</u> is <u>POWERFUL</u>.

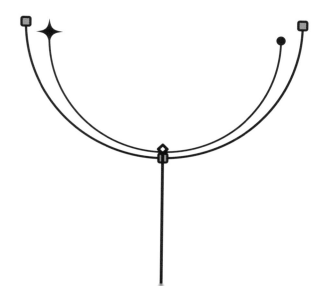

YOUR THOUGHTS AND FEELINGS BECOME YOUR REALITY.

WHAT YOU SEE, HEAR AND FEEL BECOMES YOU.

ALWAYS PROTECT YOUR MIND AND ENERGY.

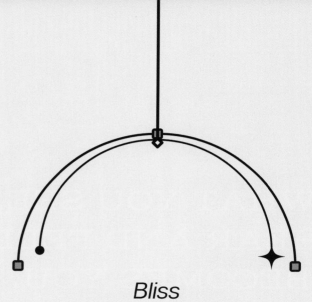

Bliss

**means your
authentic self.**

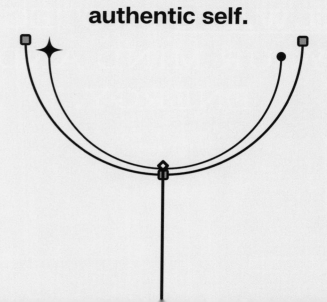

The more you take _RESPONSIBILITY_ for your actions, the more that you will get the results that you deserve.

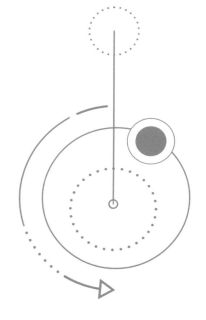

EXCHANGE YOUR
ENERGY TO WHERE
YOU WANT TO BE
AND TO WHATEVER
YOU WANT TO HAVE.

YOU CAN SHAPE
YOUR
ENVIRONMENT
BY THE WORDS
YOU SAY.

Show your
NEW VIBRATIONS.
Expect
NEW MIRACLES.